The Empowered Empath

The Ultimate Guide for Highly Sensitive People on Overcoming Anxiety, Gaining Self-confidence and Finding Your Sense of Self

By

Kasey Wittman

Table of Contents

What are Empaths?

Empaths are highly sympathizing people, who possess an avid ability to sense the thoughts and feelings of those around them. Therapists use the term *empath* to refer to people who are capable of experiencing a great amount of empathy, usually to the extent of being able to put themselves in the shoes of the other person emotionally. However, the term *empath* can also be associated with a spiritual term, describing a person with the capability to read the emotions of others.

Being an empath comes with various benefits. For example, empaths are typically amazing friends and partners. They are wonderful listeners. They are generous and big-hearted. They are always there for friends in times of need. And they are typically gifted with high intuitiveness and emotional intelligence.

However, the same qualities that make empaths such amazing friends can often take an emotional toll on empaths themselves. Since empaths are able to feel the same emotions that their friends are going through, which can cause them to be overcome with agonizing emotions, and even anxiety or trauma. Empaths often have difficulty with setting boundaries for themselves when they need to, usually when they are being overburdened with the problems of others.

Additionally, it is not uncommon for empaths to feel exhausted after being around people for a long amount of time. Empaths are typically introverts, and rely on a healthy amount of alone time so they can reenergize their body and mind, A 2011 study by the Israel Journal of Psychiatry concluded that there might be a correlation between empaths and social anxiety. Large crowds can be especially stressful for empaths, as they are typically sensitive to the loud noises and unceasing chatter. Empaths are often most at peace when surrounded by nature and natural sounds.

If you identify with these characterizes, you are more than likely an empath or have someone in your life who is, you know the struggles that come with being a highly empathetic person. Being this vulnerable to other people's pleas, emotions and energy can be incredibly taxing. For people who are just finding out about how they should deal with being empaths, knowing the pros and cons of being an empath can be very helpful. This way they can learn to know what they are in for and take care of themselves and protect their spaces and boundaries. Under certain circumstances, an empath might need to separate themselves from their empathic, or spiritual side. Giving yourself some opportunities to not be immersed in other people's problems will help with recovering their independence within their lives.

Advantages and Disadvantages of Being an Empath

Being hypersensitive is difficult to explain. It is also confusing to highlight the merits and demerits of being an empath. Being empathic can be like a two-edged sword. It can be satisfying to know intuitively you make people feel comfortable, but this can only cause you to lose your equilibrium. While taking care of others, you can easily forget about yourself. You decipher the event in your environment, but at times, it is hard to know your own mind.

Pros: You are sensitive to the emotions of others

Feeling the emotion of others is quite an amazing experience. If you see someone facing anxiety on a date or in a meeting, you can help them get better, and the rewards you can reap from this are indescribable. The number of situations where you might find this useful are endless.

Similarly, you are capable of relating to others in an exceptional manner. You truly are the exemplification of the term "to walk in another person's shoes."

This power must be properly dealt with as a result– both for yourself and those you love. However, if you can achieve this, you will unlock an incredible gift – both for yourself and your loved ones.

Cons: You sense the emotions of others

Sensing other people's emotions and being able to determine what you want to feel can be harmful and energy-sapping – both psychologically and emotionally. It confuses and overwhelms you.

You can feel other people's depression, sorrow, pain, anxiety, fear, and other emotions. You cannot control it, and this is challenging under certain circumstances.

Cons: You are susceptible to being overwhelmed

Typically, empaths are hypersensitive, as they are magnets to other people's feelings. Also, they are easily overwhelmed when they are in busy social places and around disturbing noises.

Consequently, empaths are at risk of panic attacks and being overwhelmed in noisy or busy places.

Therefore, they can experience stress when watching the news or real-life accidents. Tragic and destructive events can make them overburdened, no matter how tedious they might seem to other people.

Pros: You have amplified the ability to love and be compassionate

Empaths have an immense ability to love and be compassionate with others. In many cases, a mutual understanding is the biggest problem in a relationship.

Explaining how we feel to others does not make them really understand our feelings. It requires lots of effort and time to understand how others feel.

With the ability to feel what your loved one is feeling, you develop love and compassion. You can use this to enhance your relationship and get close to others, even people you may have differences with.

You comprehend other people's emotions and are able to compromise with them, instantly fostering a great connection that allows you to interact with others in a more peaceful and relaxed way.

Getting to Know Your Empathy Traits

Empathy represents a trait that enables people to imagine themselves in someone else's situation by picturing in their minds the feelings they might experience. Of course, there are quite a few types of empaths, all of which are characterized by unique, empathetic behavior. Getting a more in-depth understanding of your empathetic abilities can aid you in using this gift to its best potential. Below, we break down the most prevalent types of empaths listed by their frequency.

Emotional Empath

This is the most prevalent type of empath. For the most part, an emotional empath is a person that quickly absorbs the emotions of the individuals around them and experiences those emotions as their own. This type of empath stands out due to the intensity with which it can experience the feelings of others. As an example, an individual that falls in this category can easily adopt the sadness of another genuinely sad individual.

Emotional empaths need to discover how to detach their own emotions from those of others. This is the only path that can allow someone to use their empathy to aid others without diminishing their wellbeing.

Physical/ Medical Empath

A physical or medical empath can pick up the energy in other individuals. Physical empaths use their intuition to discover what upsets other persons, which is why many people in this category turn their attention towards becoming healers. This category of empaths is characterized by a powerful feeling of awareness in their bodies while healing someone. Aside from this, physical empaths can detect problems with someone's energy field if they feel like that person is in need of healing.

This type of empath can sense in his own body the ailment and symptoms that are upsetting the person next to them, which can usually lead to grave emotional distress for the empath. As such, physical empaths need to be careful controlling their emotions to prevent another person's symptoms from hurting their own wellbeing.

Geomantic Empath

This type of empath is often referred to as environmental empathy. People with geomantic empath are drawn to physical landscapes in acute ways. Aside from this, Geomantic empaths tend to experience powerful feelings of unhappiness in disturbing environments or situations without an apparent reason. Conversely, geomantic empaths might feel overjoyed in specific environments or situations that surround them with positive energy.

Overall, a geomantic empath is one that feels a deep connection to specific places or objects, such as groves, sacred stones, churches, or any other location that is said to have sacred power. Many empaths in this category can sense the history of a place or can identify past emotions. Still, the main trait of these empaths is their instinct to connect with the natural world and feel sorrow for any harmful action taken upon it.

Geomantic empaths also spend a lot of time in a natural environment, as this is the only way they can recharge with positive energy. Also, many Geomantic empaths can find healing and relief in joining environmental causes, as well as seeking to adorn their environment in as much of a peaceful atmosphere as possible, such as plants and other environmental ornaments. It is also not uncommon to see a Geomantic empath have a preference for anything that represents a connection to nature in terms of clothing, furniture, or accessories.

Plant Empath

A plant empath is a delicate individual that connects at a deeper level with the need of plants. This type of empath has a "green finger" and is gifted with the ability to find the best place in a garden (or home) for a specific plant. Many plant empaths choose to work in environments that keep them close to nature and their beloved plants.

For the most part, a plant empath thrives and longs for an environment rich in plants and trees. And it is not unusual to see an empath from this category just sitting and enjoying the presence of a majestic tree or plant. It's at these times that their soul and mind are most at peace and calm.

Animal Empath

Animal empaths are defined by a sincere inclination to nurture and care for animals. They experience a powerful connection with animals and at times more so than with humans, regardless of their breed or species. Many animal empaths choose a life dedicated to working in the field of pet care or rescue, as they seek an environment where they can express their commitment to them. Empaths in this category have a special gift: they can sense an animal's needs more so than most people.

People in this category can also occupy themselves with discovering additional information about biology and psychology concerning animals, with the simple objective of enhancing their skills of helping them. Many animal empaths eventually become animal healers, as their special skills can be used to figure out what is wrong with an animal in need and treat it accordingly.

Intuitive Empath

An intuitive empath is also referred to as a claircognizant person, as he or she can extrapolate information from individuals just by sitting next to them. An intuitive empath usually only requires a quick glance at a person to get a good read on them. Such empaths know almost instantly when someone is telling a lie, as they can identify the real intention hidden between the lines. These empaths connect at a deeper level to the energetic fields of those around them and have the power to decrypt energy to portray honesty. Somehow, this can be viewed as a similar trait to that of a **telepathic empath,** who can read thoughts.

This type of empath has a strong reliance on surrounding themselves with people that resonate with their energy, as well as an environment of strong, energetic fields, to prevent other people's thoughts and emotions from interfering with their wellbeing.

The bottom line is that being an empath is not a simple job. It comes with a plethora of powerful emotions that can create a confusing and exhausting state of mind. Still, knowing which type of empath you are can help you get control of your gift, so you always have it ready to help those around you when they most need it.

The Mirror Effect: The Reason Behind The Instant Dislike

Do you recall that moment when you attended a social gathering and someone seemed to dislike you instantly? Or that sudden outburst of resentment from a dear friend? Well, even though there is no exact reason for this shift in behavior, an empath finds it difficult to bear the brunt of such rejection from others.

Of course, this may be a common occurrence in life, as there are plenty of situations in which we feel like someone doesn't like us. Still, empaths tend to take the slightest feelings of dislike very poorly. Aside from the typical situation in which someone just isn't drawn to another person so much but doesn't necessarily object being in their presence, what is often bewildering to an empath is how certain people react in an animistic way against them when they do not understand what might have caused this.

The empath as a reflecting mirror

Many people strive to hide their own personality traits that embarrass them. And this inauthentic behavior tempts an empath to reflect those negative traits onto them. Many people try to hide parts of their personalities to manipulate others.

However, most people who go an extra step to conceal their authentic character is just striving to fit in.

The fear of judgment or hatred that comes from revealing one's true self incites many to create a false persona to hide behind. And what is even more concerning is that even sensitive personalities are prone to protect their traits from other's antipathy. In many cases, this may result in the new persona adoptee living their lives with a false identity in fear that their true persona will be disliked.

But when this type of individual gets in contact with an empath, the false persona becomes useless. The hidden traits are mirrored back at them, which automatically leads to negative thoughts directed towards the empath. Being next to an empath can bring to light any feeling, trait, or experience one desperately tries to hide. And because of this, many tend to loath empaths as soon as they meet them. Still, not many empaths have the power to realize that this intense feeling of resentment is, in reality, a mere reflection of their true self. This effect is known as the mirror of the empath.

The outburst of vibrational energy

Aside from that feeling an empath has around a negative environment, or that sudden pain or sorrow you might experience next to a negative person, many empaths are also unable to endure being around those that have outbursts of vibrational energy. An empath continuously tries to improve their skills and adopt positive changes for the mind, body, and spirit. This leads to a large amount of clean energy. But those people that experience low-level vibrations tend to dislike and avoid empaths due to their ability to vibrate clean energy.

Vibrational energy is a dominant trait for any empath, and there are plenty of people that try to avoid it. Moreover, many individuals attempt to bring down an empath by making them feel low, while others attempt to extinguish the empaths' inner-light. And when the empath is feeling down, those people might suddenly like them. But when the empath recovers their strength, a return to disliking occurs. People can sense change, no matter if it is visible or not.

Keep in mind that each individual has his own pace, meaning there is an exact time when they will be ready to increase their vibration. Many people still learn at a precise level, so they are not prepared to move forward. And due to this, they might attempt to alter an empath's outburst of vibrational energy. Hostility, negativity, and dislike are the main attitudes one can take towards an empath as a result of this clean energy.

Stillness* or quietness is not perceived as it should be

Empaths are sensitive and powerful human beings, which means they need periods of calmness. But in many situations, this tendency to get distant is perceived as disrespect from the part of the empath. Many individuals who are not at peace with themselves are inclined to assume that an empath has an arrogant or superior behavior. But the truth that many overlook is that an empath only distances himself when the emotional toll is too heavy to carry on. Empaths are individuals that act as a sponge and absorb several ailments from those in need. As a result, the need for long periods of recharging and regaining energy arises. Drained empaths want to be left alone and avoid anyone's energy field.

In such times, instant dislike or hatred can increase the agony on an empath's mental and physical wellbeing. And in this state, even small talk can be too much, which in turn can be interpreted as a clear sign of rejection. Not many individuals get a glimpse of how an empath feels daily, which is why it is so hard to understand the need for alone time. Unfortunately, the more insecure an individual is, the more inclined they are to feel offended by an empath retreating to their safe place.

How an empath can shield their energy

It is a fact that empaths can absorb other people's emotions and energy. And if empaths are in a peaceful environment filled with love, they can nourish and grow their power. Still, negative energy can have a daunting effect on an empath, which is why many empaths experience distress similar to a physical assault.

If you are an empath who aims to protect their energy stores, here are the top tips you need to know to manage clean energies as well as avoid negative energies.

How an empath can deal with their energy and remain grounded

1 Distance yourself from the negative situation or environment

The first thing you need to do is to walk away from the source of distress. It doesn't matter if you are attending a social event or not. You need to walk at least twenty feet away from the energy vampire in your midst at all costs. Being close to such a person or environment will only increase your ability to absorb negative feelings.

2 Do breathing exercises

Another efficient way to keep your energy protected from negative vibes is to breathe in and out a couple of times. Concentrating on your breath is a centering action, meaning it will create a bridge between you and your energy's core. You should avoid keeping your breath held in, as this will only prevent negativity from escaping your body.

The goal is to exhale stress and inhale calm so that you purify your energy and keep it shielded from negativity. Think about negativity as a veil lifting from your body and wellness as smooth and clear energy entering it.

3 Adopt `guerrilla meditation` practices

If you know you have to go to an event, location, or a merely crowded gathering, it is best to meditate beforehand. Reaching out to your spirit and heart will allow you to strengthen your mental and emotional traits while centering your energy and preparing it for the toll of social gatherings. It is best to start short meditation practices in the event that you feel like something is harming your wellbeing.

`Guerrilla meditation` is a five-minute break to concentrate on mindfulness and nourish positivity and love. And it can save you a lot of trouble as an empath. Your energy will be protected, while your overall state of mind will be reinforced.

4 Create constructive and healthy boundaries

Boundaries are necessary for every empath, no matter their type. So, an excellent way to keep yourself grounded and your energy clean is to limit the time spent in a stressful situation. Also, you should learn to say no to intense personality types, as they can drain you and take a toll on your wellbeing. Creating limits doesn't mean you need to explain your choice to do so if you don't want to. Remember: "no" is a complete sentence; it's a choice that protects your body, mind, and spirit from negative encounters.

5 Picture a field of energy protecting you

Visualization is a powerful tool for an empath, as it can heal the mind and body, and it is a preferred form of intrinsic protection among mental health practitioners. The key is to picture a field of energy or light surrounding and protecting your body from negative energies. If you are dealing with toxic people, you can opt for a more vivid visualization, such as a lion standing guard for your energy field.

6 Identify your needs as an empath

An empath needs to be constantly aware of their needs, so protecting one's sensitivity is key to keeping them grounded and well-balanced. To identify your needs, start by creating a list of the most intense and emotionally draining situations you experienced. Then phase out a plan for handling them — with detailed calls to action – so you can properly enact them in the moment. Put as much thought as you want into this plan; empaths can greatly benefit from intricate planning.

Mending your emotional triggers

Mending your emotional triggers means you should be compassionate and loving about your mental status. Any change in beliefs that you fostered due to the influence of friends, family, or society must be looked at with kindness. Thoughts such as "I am not good enough", or "I am too compassionate"' can take a toll on an empath's wellbeing.

You need to accept your flaws, such as any problems you have with your body image or your deservingness in finding a partner and heal from them. When you heal from these false beliefs, you achieve emotional freedom, which will prevent you from becoming emotionally triggered or exhausted in the future.

Your first trauma (or false belief) is a trigger point for you. As such, if you are angry due to an unresolved issue from the past, you might feel prone to absorb another individual's anger on the same issue as well. Or you can even experience a series of health problems due to your fear of catching another person's illness. This is why it is so vital to mend your emotional triggers, so you are less likely to soak up the emotions of others. You will still sense them, but you will not be prone to them cutting as deeply or wearing you out.

The following five approaches are a great start for dealing with your emotional triggers.

1 Awareness

The most beneficial approach you can take for mending your emotional triggers is identifying which one makes you most unbalanced. Awareness will let you discover the source of your distress while clarifying the exact issues you need to deal with and heal.

2 Trigger sources

Writing down your healing journey will allow you to pinpoint the cause of your emotional triggers. As an example, many people end up feeling unbalanced due to past experiences in which they were abused or neglected. Thus, knowing what caused your current trigger will provide additional information about your true self and why it is hurting. Keep in mind that this can be a hurtful journey, which is why it is always best to be kind to yourself. After all, you are on a healing journey meant to reveal both your ups and downs.

3 Manage negative thoughts

For this, you should take the least hurtful trigger and attempt to reprogram it. Sit in front of a mirror and talk to yourself. Tell yourself all the good things about you and your personality. Reinforce your belief that you are capable and lovable. And as you breathe gently, recite these statements out loud at least three times. Use it as a mantra to reinforce the belief that you are more than those negative thoughts.

4 Pretend you have positive thoughts

In the initial stages of your healing journey, you most likely will need to pretend you adopted an entirely positive belief. This is a good thing. For example, simply telling someone, "Not true. I did a really great job" (even if you don't entirely believe that) or "I'm proud of being sensitive. Please don't dislike me for it," conditions your mind for a deeper belief in the future. Sometimes you become more mindful so that this state of mind can harvest and become a part of you.

5. Work with a therapist or coach.

It's usually a wise choice for you to seek guidance to help you get to the bottom of the trigger and analyze the emotions involved. You might become overwhelmed with sadness or rage that your family never had any faith in you, and as a result, you never developed any faith in yourself. Expressing and liberating your emotions in healthy ways allows you to get control of your triggers and allows you to focus on your true power.

Getting control of your triggers protects you from being set off or emotionally drained by people's out of line comments. You might still find these annoying, but you will no longer be zapped by certain comments. The less power your triggers have over your emotions, the more emotionally liberated you will be.

Empaths and Relationships: Best Matches for These Unique Individuals

It's a fact everyone is looking for a soulmate. Empaths, however, have an especially difficult time achieving this goal.

At birth, empaths begin to put their emotions to use, and each one is allocated the same amount. But there are variations in the way empaths feel these emotions. Some empaths possess emotions that respond much more powerfully than others, in particular when it pertains to their romantic relationship.

The compassionate and sensitive heart of an empath can be a gift to their loved ones and those around them. But, those same traits can also cause turmoil in their relationships if they lack self-awareness and the capacity to maintain their spidey-sense. Going into a relationship in the hectic present dating world can result in an empath ending up with a broken heart or finding the love of your dreams.

Check out the following tips that can assist empaths to enjoy the world of Romance without losing control of their emotions.

A big heart – its gift and curse

Empaths are compassionate. This is not everyday compassion towards strangers. It is deep compassion and love for everyone, including those that are seemingly hard to love. In dating, this serves as a gift because it allows them to fall in love with different types of partners. When they find a willing partner, empaths can build compassionate, intentional relationships. While this may simplify love, it also comes with some risks if their compassion causes them to overlook or reduce the dangerous qualities that a partner has.

Empaths can attract the broken

Have you ever been in relationships with individuals who tend to require some healing? Such people might be closet empaths, who have yet to discover it. Or perhaps they are just facing a life crisis.

If you often date people that have not healed from problems such as trauma, abuse, or addiction, you might need to look at this pattern. Perhaps you have experienced the same problems as well and are looking for a companion with similar traits. Empaths usually have issues with codependent behaviors because of their past challenges or because they are caring and compassionate.

Spiritually, empaths are meant to assist others to heal. As well as feeling others' pain, they cannot help but assist those that require guidance and healing. You must be aware of this pattern and set boundaries to protect yourself in your relationships.

This doesn't mean you shouldn't help others in relationships. Nevertheless, you must be aware of these patterns and change them to achieve a more healthy and balanced relationship.

Determine your worth

Self-worth problems and anxiety are issues for many empaths. This is often due to their high sensitivity causing them to misinterpret the information they receive. They tend to personalize the actions and emotions of others because they connect with the feelings directly.

In addition to being self-sacrificing, empaths usually have an underlying belief of not being good enough. Along with their deep love and compassion for others, empaths often go into relationships with people who approve of their insecurities and fears. This is why it is important that you know your worth and seek partners that will do the same.

You understand an impending situation before your partner does

Empaths have the ability to know things intuitively. Once they meet a person, empaths will usually have a good understanding of what will occur in a relationship. However, if they fail to be intuitive, they may not know it is their true gut feeling.

Empaths often become too excited and quickly vulnerable after getting a slight connection with a partner. Since they understand what their partner is not aware of, empaths usually move too fast or share too much information with their partner. However, this can be threatening for a loved one that lacks the gift of empathy. So, empaths must learn to take things slowly and show feelings at the same pace as their partners.

They should also note what their intuition is saying about their partner. How many times have you overstayed in a relationship? Or you realized from the beginning you should have not dated a person, yet you did regardless. Due to the fact that empaths desire to heal and love others, they sometimes overlook the joy they deserve in life.

It is also possible for empaths to feel when something is not well with their partners. This leads to anxiety, especially if the problem is unknown or your partner cannot talk to you about it. Don't assume your feelings. Communicate with your loved one about it and work things out. Excellent communication is essential.

Safeguard yourself

Before starting any relationship, practice mindful meditation, and energetic protection exercises. These will allow you to set your boundaries (To learn about managing your empathy, check our "How Mindfulness Meditation Can Help Empaths" chapter).

You can also keep a journal to study your relationship patterns and note your intuitions. Overall, empathy can be a gift and a curse. To build a healthy, loving, and intentional relationship, know yourself and understand how you can protect yourself.

Thriving as an Empath

To many people, being empathic is a challenge. Many view additional sensitivity as something that must be eliminated or shielded to thrive nowadays. Although empaths may notice things that are easy to change about themselves, like eating habits and taking care of their bodies, more intimate aspects, like feelings and emotions, may be too difficult to handle.

After noting the powerful emotions of others, empaths may not be able to differentiate between their feelings and those projected by others. Their body assumes they are in pain, fear or sadness; hence, hormones are produced to help them cope. Handling these emotions can be hard, foggy and, at times, unbearable.

Because the majority of society is unsure as to what and who empaths are, numbing out seems to be the usual response. But becoming numb usually creates more problems for empaths. It disconnects them from their real selves and their loved ones, which unfortunately can lead to narcissism.

So what should you do? Empaths can feel the struggles and pain of those around them like a stack of bricks on their backs, yet they aren't supposed to numb out. So the next natural recourse for empaths is to shield themselves, which is another way of indirectly numbing out.

Therefore, as their last option, an empath might recuse themselves from interacting with others, become anti-social or distract themselves with bad vices like using alcohol and drugs or obsession with your phone.

When feeling better, empaths turn to beneficial techniques, like meditation, exercise, yoga, staying around positive individuals, deep breathing, and so on. They stay away from people in pain or trouble because it drains them and hurts them physically.

This is why it is recommended that you try the following techniques with the intention of mastering them as soon as possible. This will allow you to help others in the safest way possible both for yourself and your intended recipient.

Observer Consciousness

To thrive in this crazy world and maintain balance and peace, we cannot be on a constant chase for the highs of extreme excitement. As excess highs often lead to excess lows.

Rather, you should invoke a new perspective in your mind – without highs or lows. This is called neutral observer mode consciousness. It is pivotal to empaths' survival. Mindfulness meditation techniques are also essential for this. Achieve peace by being completely present, as well as get in touch with your 5 senses and maintain mental neutrality.

Neutrality allows you to view yourself as a third person without emotional sensitivity. It eliminates the fear or extremism of emotions. The sensations of feelings are higher and more intuitive. So, be neutral to differentiate intuition from emotion.

By being neutral, overactive minds are quieter and calmer. This allows you to listen to your 5 senses and think better.

Utilize daily balancing techniques, like yoga, smudging, drinking lots of water, exercise, and eating healthy to balance yourself. Afterward, be neutral so you can notice your emotions and others' emotions equally without bias.

If you can't stay neutral and find yourself viewing your emotions with ego, control yourself by pausing between action and impulses. For instance, don't scratch an itch once it is felt. Concentrate on the feeling of the itching and the desire to scratch it. First, ensure consciousness before scratching it.

This pause lets you focus on your mindfulness so that you determine your response to uncomfortable situations. This will prepare you to cope with the stronger emotions you receive.

Being neutral about the things you are surrounded by will prevent the emotions coming from others from sticking to you but rather being felt outward. Being too negative or positive makes the powerful emotions that you receive from others more impactful, thus elevating your emotions. However, when you are neutral, your emotions can flow and pass through your brain while also being sensitive enough to recognize the pain and aid in resolving it.

Similar to a shaman, healing others without losing balance can be beneficial to empaths. Afterward, they note the feelings are from others and assist them.

How to Gain Freedom from Energy Vampires

Energy vampires – Have you ever found yourself to be too consumed in helping your loved ones achieve happiness, resulting in your energy being completely depleted? If yes, this is the exact definition of an energy vampire.

Energy vampires target empaths because of their knack for helping others. The energy vampire's characteristics are manipulative, charismatic and narcissistic. As an empath, you need to understand that you cannot help a narcissist to change with appeasement and sympathy.

Ground yourself

First and foremost, you need to ground yourself. Center yourself so that the negative energies in your environment don't affect you easily. Ground yourself appropriately before dealing with an energy vampire.

You should first think about where the essence of your soul should be centered. Then think about spreading it across other parts of the body until it goes into the ground to form strong roots via your feet. The roots ensure that nothing shakes your stance. See yourself as a powerful oak tree that can hardly be uprooted.

Be with other people in a group

Dealing with an energy vampire one-on-one can affect you. However, dealing with them in a group reduces their direct effect. The pessimism of one person goes to the others as well.

This also helps you see how other people handle vampires. And as a result, you will learn how to deal with them too.

Listen to energy vampires

Most pessimistic individuals are affected by traumatic incidents in their past. Their repressed grievances may be the source of their troubles. So, listen to them. In some cases, people only need someone that can listen and be compassionate with them. They may learn how to deal with the problems after talking with others.

Only talk about light subjects

Some topics may trigger a few energy vampires. Your goal is to help them get over their negativity, and discussing certain things may trigger it. So, change the subject to ensure their mood is lightened. Talk about movies, common friends, and other things that can cheer them up.

Avoid them totally

Your last resort is cutting energy vampires from your life. This may seem extreme, but everyone cannot have a permanent presence in your life. Spending time with these negative people can drain you and result in you picking up their negative traits as well.

How to be Free From Sad Gear

Positivity is well-valued in our society. However, we are sometimes depressed on a short or long-term basis. Merely talking about the need to be positive cannot change anything because moods can act on their own. One issue with positivity is fantasizing about perfection in life, rather than understanding that nothing is perfect. Challenges, frustration, and other negative experiences are part of life.

Also, we try to distract ourselves by being passive. We spend hours browsing the internet or seeing movies, expecting the sadness to go away. However, we should be realistic, as it helps us to stop living in denial. We often rely on denial because of our inability to change the situation. However, we can do a few things to deal with sadness.

Step 1: Determine your type of sadness

Sadness consists of three types.

Short-term sadness: This only lasts for a few days or maybe a week. It may or may not have a cause. It is often caused by extreme stress, boredom, a sedentary lifestyle, and sleeplessness. To deal with this, lower your stress, sleep well, exercise constantly, and don't follow a monotonous daily routine.

Triggered sadness: This sadness comes from the occurrence of something traumatic. The occurrence may be the death of a loved one or the loss of your dream job. Hence, you understand the trigger. Despite knowing the cause, people usually feel they cannot help the situation. In this situation, consider the sadness and let others know about your feeling to get counseling and consolation. Normal people should be able to get over triggered sadness with professional therapy within six to twelve months. But if you bottle it up, it will last longer.

Depression: You may be depressed if you are helpless, sad, sleepless, hopeless, or unable to enjoy sex or eat for some weeks. Although depression usually has a trigger, it is often something you could deal with. However, depression occurs due to the breakdown of coping. This condition differs among individuals. So, you should see a therapist to deal with this.

Step 2: Getting rid of the enemies of happiness

If you are dealing with short-term and trigger sadness, you must avoid or get rid of things that might put you in a negative mood. For example, don't peg external rewards to your happiness or postpone your happiness until you achieve something in the future.

No one can make you happy except yourself. Don't overlook the signs of inner conflict and problems. Don't live in the past or be afraid of the future. Also, understand that momentary pleasure is different from happiness.

Nowadays, everything is about consumerism. And we can easily do all those things we ought to avoid. Nevertheless, you must understand how you can develop a feeling of happiness because you are responsible for your happiness. Although being happy requires a lot of effort, each step is fulfilling.

Step 3: Develop wellbeing

If you accept your sadness passively, you are essentially negating the development of your happiness. Happiness goes beyond a mood. It requires a long-term condition that is known as wellbeing, which involves a balanced body and mind that is felt in the form of emotional freedom, peace of mind, and satisfaction. A few things you can do include helping others, partaking in physical activity, pursuing long-term goals, and exploring new possibilities, leaving your past behind, looking forward to the future, having good social interactions, and being resilient.

Being resilient emotionally is probably more essential than other traits because it helps you get back on your feet after bad occurrences. You can be resilient by living in the present without fears and past victimizations, by dealing with any wrong happenings directly, staying around emotionally mature individuals, considering how you have coped in the past, and rewarding yourself for surpassing tough trials and tribulations.

Emotionally mature happiness goes a long way in protecting you against bad moods. Sadness never lasts, but wellbeing can.

Letting go of Suffering and Finding Acceptance

Holding on to the past is a natural human flaw that keeps us from achieving our goals. Keeping memories with us in a relationship that replays in our minds, we all do it, such as an old grudge from a malicious remark from a friend. So, why do we have such trouble letting these memories go? The reason is because we are conditioned to hold on to things because, in part, it's satisfying. Familiarity and justification are comforting, even when it's attached to a painful experience. But, in the end, there is no benefit to not learning how to let go – it only keeps you from reaching your real potential.

In order to learn to live proactively and positively, you need to let go. Probably the most emotionally taxing thing to let go of is past relationships. The idea of erasing someone whom you have shared your life with and developed a strong bond is a heavy burden. However, it is something you will need to do in order to find the liberation you need to thrive in life. The question is, are you willing to change a part of yourself and let go of past memories that do you more harm than good?

Here are some tips to redirect your painful thoughts into something positive.

Mind control can break the cycle of the unhealthy obsession of these thoughts, ideas, and feelings. The human mind is very complicated to control, and it can sometimes be our worst enemy or greatest ally. Having the ability to move on from things begins there.

For most people, when their mind rehearses a dark or painful experience, they come to conclusions such as "I'm unlovable" and "No one cares about me". The more you repeat these thoughts to yourself, the more you will end up resenting yourself and allowing frustration and anger to fester and completely shape your personality.

The truth is your value is not determined by your thoughts. You do not have to be shaped by your life experiences. Just because something doesn't go in your favor doesn't mean you are doomed to failure and incapable of achieving everything you want in life.

The more we can simply watch our thoughts come and go, the more we moderate how our thoughts come and go without making them part of our identity, the easier it becomes simpler to let them go.

Getting it all out

Being in control of your emotions in a healthy way is an important step to analyzing them prior to letting them go. This is why I also recommend that you take the time to journal your thoughts and emotions.

While being obsessed with every detail that occurred in the past is never good for our mental health, it's important to process them and find out why they're making you feel sad or angry and how you can turn that into a positive memory in the future.

Self-reflection allows us to achieve a wide variety of breakthroughs. Other ways to help spill out your thoughts include talking to a trusted family member or friend or therapist. Professional consulting, in particular, is one of the best ways to experience objective advice and encouragement during your healing journey and learn the art of letting go.

When we attach ourselves to pain, anxiety, resentment, and grief from past experiences without fully processing them, each one of these feelings accumulates within our heart, making it an even bigger challenge to let them go. When this happens, it's best to seek help from a therapist to guide you through the healing process from within yourself.

Acceptance

Everybody wants to get to the bottom of why something ended badly or how a person could be able to hurt us so badly without caring about how it would negatively affect our lives.

We obsess over finding an explanation for these answers. We need some sort of rationalization. The sad truth is that the "closure" we think we deserve doesn't always arrive no matter how much we want it.

Not everyone is willing to admit they did something wrong and take the blame for the damage they caused you. And this can sometimes make a situation worse and seem like they are pouring salt on an open wound.

The only way to get on the right path to mental well-being is by fully accepting the situation for what it is without constantly hoping it will change. And this isn't limited to coming to peace with certain situations. We need to start accepting people for their flaws and believing them when their true character comes out. Because they are telling the truth.

Forgiveness

In order to let go of a situation, sometimes forgiving those who won't apologize is necessary. Sometimes you need to come to terms that you will never receive an apology, and that's OK. This commitment takes so much courage and strength and might seem unfair to you and even backwards, but in many cases that's the lengths you need to go to come to peace with yourself.

There's nothing that causes us more emotional pain than holding onto personal grudges for years, while the person you are holding it against has moved on with their life. And the truth is that resentment only hurts *you.* When we learn to forgive others, we benefit from the very important part of forgiving ourselves.

This can be done by journaling your thoughts and replacing self-loathing with sympathy and chronicling your plans to make better choices next time.

How Mindfulness Meditation Can Help Empaths

In the past few years, more psychologists and other mental health professionals have included mindfulness meditation in their therapy sessions. Mindfulness meditation is effective for various mental illnesses, including anxiety disorder, chronic pain, major depressive disorder, and borderline personality disorder.

What Is Mindfulness Meditation?

The purpose of mindfulness mediation is about living your day to day life without casting judgment on others and being very considerate.

When you are in a state of mindfulness meditation, you condition yourself not to think about the past or future but focus on the moment. You practice focusing on being aware of your surroundings, such as the things you smell and touch and the sensations you experience.

Because the purpose of mindfulness is about eliminating judgment, you are to see these things through a neutral perspective.

What are the connections between Mindfulness Meditation and Empaths?

Often, Empaths who practice Mindfulness Meditation not only experience overwhelming emotions, but they also hold on to these emotions and end up judging both emotions and themselves.

Unfortunately, this can result in intensifying our emotions. Judgmental thoughts can bring about other emotions. If you convince yourself that you are feeling sad and weak, the natural reaction from your brain and body will be to feel both sad and feeble.

Empaths can accept mindfulness meditation to help them apply healthy coping skills to handle overwhelming emotional pain. Mindfulness allows you to achieve a more open mind to be able to think strategically on how you will react in the presence of emotion.

For example, imagine partaking in a heated argument with your significant other. Throughout the argument, you might experience intense feelings, such as fear, anger, and rage. Without using mindfulness, you might ignore the consequences of your actions and act irresponsibly. You may make an uncalled for remark, fling something at them, or storm out.

With mindfulness skills, you will learn to recognize the emotions you are experiencing and learn to stop yourself and act out your behavior appropriately, such as taking a break until you are able to discuss things calmly.

Practicing mindfulness for PTSD might be a healthy coping method. People with PTSD might, at times, feel as though they have difficulties staying away from unpleasant memories and thoughts. And as a result, many of those with PTSD often have trouble concentrating their attention on things that matter in their life, like family and relationships or the daily activities that used to bring them joy.

Studies on Mindfulness and PTSD

Mindfulness therapy's goal is to help divert a person from their overly engaged thinking patterns and emotional distress.

A study published this year in the *Journal of The American Medical Association* found soldiers on return duty who had partaken in mindful-based therapies experienced a drastic decline in PTSD symptoms in the short-term, compared to those who underwent other traditional therapies for depression and anxiety.

This study consisted of 58 veterans with PTSD undergoing 9 mindful-based stress reduction sessions, while 58 others went through a therapy focused on resolving daily problems, called control therapy. After the treatment, people in the mindfulness group had a 49% reduction of their symptoms, while those in the control therapy group saw a drop of 28%.

However, after a follow-up two months later, these groups still did not lose the PTSD diagnosis. Therefore, even though the study concluded that the approach might work in the short-term, further work is needed to bring about its real benefits compared to other trauma-focused approaches.

While mindfulness-based therapies aren't a sufficient replacement for current trauma-based psychological treatments that are backed by a substantial amount of evidence, they might be useful in more extensive treatment plans. They previously have been shown to be potent for common, non-traumatic depressive and anxiety disorders and, worth noting, resonates with a lot of patients.

Starting a Mindfulness Meditation Practice

Practicing mindfulness meditation is an easy and straightforward process that anyone can do, but if you are having trouble following through, you can find a teacher or program to help you get on the right track, especially if you are doing meditation for mental health reasons.

Every bit of practice can make a difference. Here's a simple technique you can use to get started:

- Find a comfortable and silent place. Sit down on a chair or on the ground with your head and back straight and relaxed. It's also recommended to wear comfortable clothing that doesn't distract you.

- Set aside all past and future thoughts and focus on the present.

- Take control of your breath, tuning in to the feeling of air flowing in and out of your body every time you breathe. Feel the air enter your nostrils and leave your mouth as your belly falls and rises. Focus on each breath and how they are changing.

- See every thought come in and out, whether it be anxiety, fear, or hope. When you come up with a thought, don't ignore or restrain them. Simply notice them, stay calm, and control them with your breath.

Be nice to your wandering mind

During your mediation, you will find your mind constantly wandering – this is completely normal. Rather than suppressing these thoughts, practice focusing on them through a neutral lens. Just sit without reacting. As hard as this might be, that's the best thing you can do. Return to your breath a couple of times, without expectation or judgment.

If you find that your thoughts are getting too intense, figure out where your mind went, with a neutral mindset, and resume your breathing exercises. Remember to be as relaxed as possible if this happens.

As you feel your session coming to an end, sit for another minute and analyze where you are. Get up gradually. In the beginning, it's important to meditate on a daily basis. That means you can practice as long as you want.

After a while, you'll feel gradually able to sit for longer periods.

Practice x2 a day.

For the first 1-3 weeks, practice mindful breathing for 1-3 minutes. This is the most important step when getting started, and even with this single step, you will notice a great improvement in your mood and overall health. After a while of practice and conditioning, you will be able to sit for longer periods of time.

To develop increasingly your mindfulness meditation regimen and turn it into a powerful daily practice, sit twice a day (preferably at morning first, then afternoon or night). Keep in mind that you are only taking 1-3 minutes out of your day, so you have no excuse not to do so.)

Your mind will be in a tailspin. Don't sweat it.

Newcomers to meditation often feel like they are approaching it wrong or that they are not fit for it. The truth is these feelings are very common and natural. It's perfectly normal to feel like you are about to go crazy, unable to keep your mind on a single point for more than a few seconds. This will gradually change for the better as long as you are dedicated to your daily practice regimen.

Go easy on yourself throughout the process

Don't approach mindfulness meditation expecting that it will be easy. For most people, it isn't. When you are starting, more than likely, you will not clearly notice what is developing. You'll feel like you lost your mindfulness. At most, you'll recognize that you were having thoughts about "something" without knowing exactly what. But there is a chance that a few unpleasant thoughts might come to you while meditating. Don't be hard on yourself and know that affliction is just part of the learning process and not a personal shortcoming.

Practicing mindfulness for PTSD might be a healthy coping method. People with PTSD might, at times, feel as though they have difficulties straying away from unpleasant memories and thoughts. And as a result, many of those with PTSD often have trouble concentrating their attention on things that matter in their life, like family and relationships or the daily activities that used to bring them joy.

Studies on Mindfulness and PTSD

Mindfulness therapy's goal is to help divert a person away from their overly engaged thinking patterns and emotional distress.

A study published this year in the *Journal of The American Medical Association* found soldiers on return duty who had partaken in mindful-based therapies experienced a drastic decline in PTSD symptoms in the short term, compared to those who underwent other traditional therapies for depression and anxiety.

This study consisted of 58 veterans with PTSD undergoing 9 mindful-based stress reduction sessions, while 58 others went through a therapy focused on resolving daily problems called control therapy. After the treatment, people in the mindfulness group had a 49% reduction of their symptoms, while those in the control therapy group saw a drop of 28%.

However, after a follow-up two months later, these groups still did not lose the PTSD diagnosis. Therefore, even though the study concluded that the approach might work in the short-term, further work is needed to bring about its real benefits compared to other trauma-focused approaches.

While mindfulness-based therapies aren't a sufficient replacement for current trauma-based psychological treatments, which are backed by a substantial amount of evidence, they might be useful in more extensive treatment plans. They previously have been shown to be potent for common, non-traumatic depressive and anxiety disorders, and worth noting resonates with a lot of patients.

Incorporating Mindfulness into Your Daily Life

Believe it or not, mindfulness meditation is not the only technique you can use to achieve mindfulness. You can add mindfulness practices to your daily activities and tasks, which will provide plenty of practice opportunities.

Here are some tips on cultivating mindfulness in your everyday routine.

Washing the Dishes

Have you ever noticed how you are always laser-focused on the task at hand when you are doing the dishes? The combination of solidarity and repetitive physical labor makes dinner clean-up a perfect time to practice a little mindfulness. Indulge in the feeling of warm water soaking your hands, the sounds of the pans clanking on the bottom of the sink, and the soaring bubbles.

Condition your mind to enjoy the task at hand, not try to get it over with as quickly as possible so you can watch your favorite TV show. When you immerse yourself in the moment, you achieve the mental rejuvenation and great results of your chore.

Increase your awareness & engage senses

Encourage yourself to go on a brisk walk every day and focus your attention on the majestic beauty of nature and the environment. Lone walks are greatly invigorating. It has been shown to improve your heart's health, lower heart disease, and boost your mood.

During your walk, be in control of your senses closing in on each sight, smell, sound, and sensation. Embrace mother nature's majesty around you; experience each moment slowly and as it is. Feel the titillating gleam of sunshine on your face; let the fragrance of fresh flowers sweep you away as the breezy wind flutters through your hair. A simple walk can become a truly enchanting experience.

Don't miss this opportunity to disconnect from your gadgets and devices and be one with nature. Research has shown that it unlocks positive emotions and puts our parasympathetic nervous system in motion, which restores and calms us. Nature is our home. Don't hesitate to fuse the infinite benefits of mindfulness and immerse yourself in mother nature.

Eating

We are all guilty of urgently going through our lunch break. Be present in the moment and indulge every burst of flavor every delectable bite contains. Mealtime should be savored with diligence, not rushed. When done properly, food can nurture the mind, body, and soul, as well as bring out your senses and activate your mind.

When indulging in your meal, find the quietest and serene area, be in the moment, and focus as you peacefully and carefully enjoy your food. Be sure to ignore your electronic devices. Around you, you will see and enjoy textures, smells, and bursting flavors like you've never experienced, making every bite an utter delight. This level of positivity will become part of you and follow you into every facet of your everyday life.

Wake up well

Most people are guilty of waking up in a bad mood to the sound of a phone alarm, checking the news and Instagram notifications before haltingly popping out of bed. Well, it doesn't have to be this way! Switch your alarm ringtone to a more blissful, soothing sound. Set it to a minimum of 30 minutes earlier than normal. This will give you time to wake up gradually and peacefully. Be sure to be attentive of your body waking up, stretch your arms and legs, wiggle your fingers and toes, and take a few deep inhales and exhales and start the day with a positive mindset.

After getting out of bed, make yourself some hot tea with lemon and an alkalizing fruit and get on your yoga mat to start moving your body with a few sessions of sun salutations and meditation. If you are feeling more energetic, you can go for a short morning walk, which is a fantastic way to de-clutter your head. Whichever way you choose to remedy your morning blues, allow yourself to let that inspiration follow you throughout the day. This conventional change in your morning routine will foster positive energy and gratefulness for the remainder of the day and eventually your life.

Self-Love

Last but definitely not least, and sadly in many cases, you need to remind yourself you are worthy of self-love. It is essential to prioritize yourself and use a bit of selfishness in your daily life. Self-love can be applied in many forms, like assembling a stunning outfit that makes you feel invincible with self-confidence, as long as in the end it is making YOU happy.

It's no secret self-love is easier said than done. Figure out simple things you love about yourself and want to protect or improve. You can make a few adjustments, like planning a spa day once every two weeks or allowing yourself to get a full 10 hours of rest a night. Then start cutting down on time wasted using the internet or watching TV and take the smarter approach of reading a book and getting to know yourself. Most importantly, make every day you live purposeful by becoming mindful in all aspects of life.

Your aim should be to practice mindfulness daily for around six months. As time passes, you may learn to use your mindfulness

without any effort. Think of it as a process of nurturing and
reconnecting with yourself.

There you have it. You are now well on your way to finally achieving peace and mastering the power of being an Empath forever!

Be prepared to live a life filled with positivity, feel great and achieve the goals you always strived for in life! Thank you for taking the time to read my book and stay tuned for more books on self-help in the future.

If you enjoyed my book and would recommend it to anyone. I'd be very grateful if you can leave a short review on Amazon. Your feedback is really important, and I will use the opportunity to further improve this book even more in the future.

Thanks again for your support!